CONTENTS

HOW TO USE THIS BOOK

Who is your group?

This book is intentionally aimed at mixed groups - families, missional communities, All Age services and other places where young and older meet. These are ideal spaces to engage playfully, creatively and actively with God's creation, as his diverse body. We can learn from one another and be surprised by what we see from another person's perspective.

However, this breadth means you need to consider your group and tailor each of our activities to suit the ages and abilities present. Read them through and think about what will work with the people you're leading. We've tried to give suggestions for "going deeper", but you are ultimately the best judge of whether your group needs more or less playing, talking, prayer, creating and so on.

Where are you?

Another thing about an "outdoor" book is that it depends a lot on the spaces you have available to you. We've lived in the countryside as well as in built-up London and Luton, and have found that there are always parks, gardens, trees, rivers and wildlife to be found if you look hard enough.

Yet it is true that in some areas you'll be able to find these easier than in others. So scout out your locations before settling on an idea.

What is the weather like?

Sara's home country of Sweden has a phrase - "there are no bad weathers, only bad clothes" (it rhymes in Swedish...). Sometimes we might need to get a bit braver and enjoy God's creation in wind, rain and overcast skies. Different seasons of the year have different experiences to offer. But do bear the weather in mind when planning your activities, and perhaps invest in a good raincoat.

Break down the walls...

In contemporary church we often separate "worship" from "everyday life". In this book we have intentionally blurred the boundaries between what might be considered "leisure activities" and "spiritual practices". Embrace this! For some reading this book, it will transform your walk to work or school, your holiday, or your Saturday afternoon. For others, it will take your home group, Sunday service or youth meeting out of doors and into God's creation. Whatever your context, enjoy engaging with God in his world.

WHY WORSHIP OUTDOORS?

"Nature makes you nicer!"

The work we do in the 21st century mostly does not relate to digging over soil or herding animals. It requires us instead to be near an electrical outlet, in order to plug in all our digital devices and to keep good access to the Internet. The children and young people around us need to be indoors a lot too - that is where their classrooms are situated, and they also need computer access for homework.

If we are honest, many of us choose screens over going outside if given the option. When our son was younger, he would tell us that he was feeling hungry or thirsty, but he also added his own need: "Mummy, I'm feeling screeny!"

And yet, scientists, psychologists and behavioural experts keep finding the same research results - humans need to be outside. It's vital for our physical and mental well-being; it makes us healthier, smarter and as mentioned above, nicer.

www.nwf.org/What-We-Do/Kids-and-Nature/Why-Get-Kids-Outside/Health-Benefits.aspx and www.theguardian.com/lifeandstyle/2010/aug/16/childre-nature-outside-play-health

This is the kind of science that simply underlines what most of us already knew. We feel calmer when we take a walk in nature; many of us choose holidays that involve the outdoors (whether that is camping, lying on a beach or hiking); and if you have kids or work with kids you will know how much easier childcare is in an outdoor, natural environment. There they have space to roam, use their bodies to their full capacities and

explore with all their senses. Many people of faith will also feel a special connection with God in nature. This seems logical if you believe in a God who thought all these things up - his fingerprints are over everything!

People who study the Bible and try to understand more about God call this "natural theology". This is the idea that anybody can learn about God by observing the natural world. One theologian, Alister McGrath, defines natural theology as an "open secret" - something that is available for everyone, but "...whose true meaning is known only from the standpoint of Christian faith."

Alister E. McGrath, The Open Secret: A New Vision for Natural Theology (2008) page 11.

What a wonderful opportunity we have then, to learn about and worship God, with one eye on Scripture and one eye on the natural world around us. "Since the creation of the world God's invisible qualities – his eternal power and divine nature – have been clearly seen, being understood from what has been made..." (Romans 1:20)

This is what this book is about. We want to encourage you to take your worship outdoors - not only will being outdoors make you healthier, smarter and nicer if you believe the experts, but the very environment you are in will reveal something about the God you worship.

Someone who understood this from an early age was the wonderful character of Anne of Green Gables, thought up by L.M. Montgomery, and I would like to finish this introduction with a quote from her lips on being taught how to pray:

"Why must people kneel down to pray? If I really wanted to pray I'll tell you what I'd do. I'd go out into a great big field all alone or into the deep, deep, woods, and I'd look up into the sky - up - up - up - into that lovely blue sky that looks as if there was no end to its blueness. And then I'd just feel a prayer."

GATHERING LEAVES

> *"That person is like a tree planted by streams of water, which yields its fruit in season and whose leaf does not wither — whatever they do prospers."*
> Psalm 1:3

Activity

When you are in woodland, see how many different leaves you can find, and collect them (try to pick from the ground rather than from the tree itself). Spread the leaves out on a white sheet and talk about how they are different. Compare the shapes and set challenges, eg: find the roundest, longest, softest or hardest ones. If you have picked leaves or needles from ever-greens, talk about how they are different from leaves of deciduous trees (those that shed their leaves in autumn time).

Choose a leaf to make a leaf rubbing, by placing the paper on top of the leaf and evenly colouring with the crayon on top. The outline and veins of the leaf should come out in a stronger colour. Explain how trees need water and sunlight to survive. In the autumn when there are less sun-hours, the tree protects itself by shedding its leaves and focusing on simply surviving as a trunk with branches.

You will need

A white sheet
Access to woodland
Crayons, paper

Going Deeper

Read Psalm 1:1-3. Discuss how the psalm says that if we follow God, and spend time meditating on his Word, we are like trees that do not need to conserve energy - we can be full of life in all seasons, like a tree whose leaves never wither.

Discuss: 1) The psalm talks about "fruit in season" - what kind of fruit can Christians bear? 2) How do you meditate on God's word? The writer of this psalm says it's good to meditate day and night - which time of day do you find easiest to spend with God?

Worship Response

Do some meditating on God's word. Try to sit or lie as quietly as possible as one person reads Psalm 1:1-3 slowly out loud, 3-4 times. Ask everyone which word stands out to them, then ask them to repeat that word quietly in their heart for a minute. Finish with a prayer thanking God for being present and speaking through his word.

Stick your leaf rubbings in here

BURIED SEEDS

> "Very truly I tell you, unless a grain of wheat falls to the ground and dies, it remains only a single seed. But if it dies, it produces many seeds. Anyone who loves their life will lose it, while anyone who hates their life in this world will keep it for eternal life."
> John 12:24-25

Activity

Give everyone a seed to hold in their hand. Ask the group to suggest describing words for the seed. Next, look at the picture on the seed packet - what are some describing words to use for the plant that is on the picture? Compare the seed and the plant on the picture, how are they different. Explain that the attitude with which we plant seeds can be described as "hope". We cannot be sure that the seed will take root, or that it will turn out just like on the picture, but when we plant the seed we hope that it will. Go ahead and plant your seed at this point by filling a pot with soil and following the instructions on the seed packet.

Explain that God gives us hope in our lives, even when things look bad (like the dark soil of the buried seed), we can hope that God will bring about good things. Do not forget to keep watering the soil in the coming days!

You will need

Small pots
Potting compost
Seeds (for example sunflower or radish) and their packets
Water

Going Deeper

Read John 12:25 together and discuss: Are there things in your life that you are holding onto, but that you need to lay down before Jesus before they can bear fruit? This could be, for example, personal hopes, relationships, work, ministry etc.

Imagine this thing being the seed and allow it to "die" and be buried - in the act of planting, hand the issue to Jesus and ask his will to be done. Pray that your planted issue will bear fruit.

Worship Response

Tie or glue together a simple cross using two sticks (or even pipe cleaners for simplicity), and place it in the soil. Explain that Jesus allowed himself to die and be buried, just like the seed. Take turns thanking Jesus for his death on the cross, or perhaps sing a song on a cross theme.

seeds of...

write or draw below the things you are hoping for

FIRSTFRUITS

> *"But Christ has indeed been raised from the dead, the firstfruits of those who have fallen asleep. For since death came through a man, the resurrection of the dead comes also through a man. For as in Adam all die, so in Christ all will be made alive."*
> 1 Corinthians 15:20-22

You will need

The pot from "Buried Seeds" activity, hopefully with some growth!

Activity

When the seed from the 'Buried Seed' activity has grown up, discuss:
1. At first, did the pot look more like a picture of "death" or of "life"?
2. Were you good at remembering to water the pot? Was it hard to feel excited about watering the pot before the plant came up?
3. Does the plant as it looks now make you think more about the word "death" or the word "life"?

Look at the cross in your pot and remind the group that you had been thinking about Jesus' death and new life. Share that the Bible calls Jesus' resurrection "firstfruits". What do people think that means? Discuss the idea that Jesus is the first of many, and that when we belong to him we can also trust in eternal life.

Going Deeper

Discuss the group's definition of resurrection or eternal life: do we expect "pie in the sky when we die" or could it be something we have already entered into? What are signs of resurrection in yours and others' lives right now?

When Jesus teaches us to pray, he prays for the Kingdom to come not just in heaven, but also on earth. Perhaps pray the Lord's prayer together, pausing to add places on earth when you want to see God's Kingdom breaking through.

Worship Response

Take turns thanking God for signs of new life in your own experiences, glimpses of his Kingdom reign all around you. Perhaps sing a song about Jesus' resurrection (for example, "The Greatest Day in History" (Tim Hughes) or "Thine Be The Glory" (Edmond Budry, trans Richard Birch Hoyle).)

Draw or stick in a picture of your plants

BREAD & FIRE

"Jesus declared, "I am the bread of life. Whoever comes to me will never go hungry, and whoever believes in me will never be thirsty."
John 6:35

Activity

Build a fire or barbecue and have an adult light it. Carefully whittle all around the top of the sticks with a sharp knife to reveal the clean wood inside. Roll a dough ball into a long, thin snake shape. Next coil the dough over the clean part of the stick, ensuring that the dough is neatly tucked into itself top and bottom.

Cook the bread over glowing embers (flames are too hot!), constantly turning it over to get an even bake. When cooked, the bread is delicious brushed with a bit of butter and dipped in a sugar and cinnamon mix.

As the bread cooks, talk about all the different kinds of bread you know of - who can list the most kinds? Which countries do the different breads come from? Marvel at how people all over the world have worked out their favourite way to make bread.

Talk about how Jesus called himself "the bread of life", but that he had to be broken to give us life. He died on the cross to take our punishment for sin. This is why we break bread when we celebrate Communion, or the Lord's Supper - we remember that Jesus' body was broken to give us life. This life is more that just the life that we get from eating food (survival), but a life that goes on forever.

You will need

Ingredients for a bread dough:
- 240g plain flour
- 1 tsp salt
- 1 tsp baking powder
- 50ml oil or melted butter
- 150ml milk
(Combine these at home, divide into 12 balls and carry in an air-proof container)

Long fresh sticks

A sharp knife

The things you need to light a barbecue or fire pit

Going Deeper

Bring along wine or grape juice, and celebrate the Lord's Supper together when the bread has cooked.

Worship Response

Take the first bread that is finished, break it and share it out. You might want to pray something like: *"Thank you Jesus that you were broken so that I can have real life. Thank you that you are the bread of life, Amen".*

RUBBISH

> *"The Lord God took the man and put him in the Garden of Eden to work it and take care of it."*
> Genesis 2:15

Activity

Go for a rubbish-picking walk. With children and teenagers, talk about safety and what to avoid touching with their hands. As you pick, discuss what different rubbish you find and why someone might have left it there.

Over a picnic (time to get that hand sanitiser out!), talk about what rubbish does to nature - how can it be dangerous to us or animals? How can it be bad for the environment at large? As Christians, how should we respond?

Discuss how in the story of Creation, God creates the human beings to look after the freshly made earth. How can we do this? (eg: dealing with rubbish, trying to use less packaging, using products with less toxins in, etc).

Think also about humans, who are part of creation and who we should also care for. Look at the rubbish you have collected, and try to think with compassion about the people who have left it behind - what problems and struggles might be the cause of the rubbish being left?

You will need

Bin bags
Gardening gloves
Rubbish pickers
(some councils have these to lend)
Picnic
Hand sanitiser

Going Deeper

Engage in some guerrilla gardening: find a desolate looking place in your area and plant some things are are good for the environment - for example, plants that attract bees and butterflies, or simply make a big visual impact. Make a difference in the world!

Worship Response

Spend some time looking at the rubbish you've collected, and pray for the people who left it there - God knows and loves them. Perhaps end with some silence, where everyone can have a chance to think about how they can follow God's direction to care for the earth.

Draw the place you tidied in its new clean form

TREASURE HUNT

> *"The kingdom of heaven is like treasure hidden in a field. When a man found it, he hid it again, and then in his joy went and sold all he had and bought that field."* Matthew 13:44

Activity

Have a go at geocaching, which is a worldwide treasure hunt game. Visit the website, and then use GPS and the clues to find a treasure that someone else has left. Leave a note and some inexpensive trinket in there, and (if you leave something) take a souvenir from the cache.

When you have found the cache, retell Jesus' parable from Matthew 13:44. Make it into a proper story with characters and descriptions of the treasure.

Discuss the area where you have been geocaching - how much would it cost to buy the land? What kind of treasure would there have to have been in the geocache for you to sell everything you owned to buy the land (precious metals or jewels, a painting by a Master etc)? What would be worth getting rid of your house / car / phones etc for? Explain that Jesus describes 'the Kingdom of God' as that kind of treasure - that is worth leaving everything for. The really good news is that we are invited into this Kingdom completely for free!

You will need

Internet access (www.geocaching.com) A GPS enabled phone

Going Deeper

What would be a blessing for someone to find in a geocache? An encouraging note, a nicer than usual trinket, a book?

Create and hide your own cache to bless the geocaching community in your area.

Worship Response

Pray a prayer thanking King Jesus that we are invited into his Kingdom for free. Perhaps give opportunity for anyone who has not yet invited Jesus to be King in their lives to do so.

Create a treasure map showing where you walked,
and an X to mark the spot!

CLOUD SPOTTING

> "The heavens declare the glory of God;
> the skies proclaim the work of his hands.
> Day after day they pour forth speech;
> night after night they reveal knowledge."
> Psalm 19:1-2

You will need

A day with just enough clouds
A cloud spotting guide or app
A blanket
Binoculars (not essential)

Going Deeper

Get hold of a cloud spotter's guide, print a guide out from the Internet or download a cloud spotting app. Engage in some serious analysis of the sky - can you tell a Cirrus cloud apart from a Cumulus one?

Psalm 19 is a wonderfully creative song about how the sky gives glory to God, showing his nature. Why not have a go at re-writing the psalm in your own words, using your experience of looking up at the clouds? You could do it as a rhyming or free poem, a rap, a song, or in any other format!

Activity

Spend some lazy time on your back, looking at clouds. Talk to each other about what you think the clouds look like. Ask questions like: which is the smallest cloud I can see? Which is the largest? Which cloud looks angriest? Which looks happiest? Or whatever questions you can think of to stir up imagination.

Worship Response

Psalm 19 says that the heavens declare the glory of the Lord – talk about what in particular might be glorious about the sky on this particular day. Ask everyone to look out for an image in the cloud that reminds them of something about God, and have a moment's silence. Then, as an act of worship, encourage everyone to share what they have been reminded of.

Draw the different clouds here

NATURE SINGING

> "Let the heavens rejoice, let the earth be glad;
> let the sea resound, and all that is in it.
> Let the fields be jubilant, and everything in them;
> let all the trees of the forest sing for joy.
> Let all creation rejoice before the Lord..." Psalm 96:11-13a

Activity

Use this idea when you are by the sea, near a field of ripe grains or in a forest. Ask everyone to make themselves comfortable or a blanket or similar.

Read the whole of Psalm 96 out loud. Explain that in this psalm "all the earth" is encouraged to "sing to the Lord," and that it goes on to list a few things in nature that "sing" (or at least make noise!) - can anyone remember what they were?

Take a moment to listen to the earth's "sung" worship - get comfortable and stay as still and quiet as you can. Listen really carefully to what you can hear - can you identify where all the noises come from? Does it have some sort of rhythm to it?

You will need

An undisturbed space in nature
A blanket

Going Deeper

Discuss the following questions: How do we as humans try to control or hinder the earth's natural worship? What would it look like if all of creation had the opportunity to fully "rejoice before the Lord" (v13a)?

Read the final verse of the psalm and discuss what God's judgment may have to do with the previous verses.

Worship Response

Try to copy the natural sounds you hear - imagine that you are the trees, the sea or the fields resounding and add background noise to one person reading the psalm out loud.

For the under 5s, Julia Plaut's song "Mr Cow" would be useful in this activity - as well as considering how cows and sheep worship God, add some verses about waves, trees and wind.

For an older group, songs like "Indescribable" (Jesse Reeves, Laura Story) or hymns like "Great is thy Faithfulness" (Thomas Chisholm) could be sung.

MOTHER HEN

> "...how often I have longed to gather your children together, as a hen gathers her chicks under her wings, and you were not willing."
> Luke 13:34

You will need

Hens to observe

Activity

This activity might be suitable in the event of a farm visit or a trip to a petting zoo, but it is also not uncommon for city dwellers to keep a couple of chickens in their back garden. Spend some time observing the hens. Explain that Jesus cried over the people who lived in Jerusalem, and longed to gather them safely, like a hen gathers her chicks under her wings.

Although you are unlikely to witness any hen gathering her chicks, spend some time reflecting on the image that Jesus used:
1. Which words would you use to describe the hen's wings? Perhaps do a sketch of the wing.
2. Why do you think the hen would gather her chicks under her wings?
3. If you were a chick, how would you feel about being held under your mother hen's wing?

Going Deeper

Jesus used "mothering" language to describe his emotion. Generally, God reveals himself as Father in Scripture - but are there aspects of his character that are more traditionally associated with mothers? Can you think of other Biblical examples of God taking on more of a mother role?

Draw the hen here

Worship Response

Hold your arms out pretending they are big wings. Wrap them around yourself whilst saying this short prayer: "God, gather me, keep me safe and hold me close, like the mother hen holds her chicks. Amen."

PERSPECTIVES

> *"The Lord does not look at the things people look at. People look at the outward appearance, but the Lord looks at the heart."*
> 1 Samuel 16:7b

You will need

A magnifying glass (you could also do something similar with binoculars)

Activity

Spend some time enjoying the different perspectives that a magnifying glass gives you. On the next page, do a drawing of a plant or an insect with and without the magnifying glass. Marvel at how much more you can see using these instruments.

Discuss how just as we get a different perspective when we use a magnifying glass, so God has a different perspective when he looks at people. He can see what is going on inside a person.

Worship Response

Think quietly about anyone that you know that you have judged in the past - perhaps because they behave in a mean way, or even because of how they look.

Pray that God will help you see that person differently, as if looking through God's magnifying glass, and that you will see all the good things in that person, all those things that God loves.

Going Deeper

Discuss: how much can you know about someone by looking at their outside? What things are you tempted to judge people on: their clothes, hair, job title, posessions...?

We can ask God to give us his perspective on people, especially if we have people in our lives whom we struggle with - God knows why they behave as they do.

Draw your object without a magnifying glass

Now draw a detail you see through the glass

BIRD WATCHING

> *"...and the Holy Spirit descended on him in bodily form like a dove."* Luke 3:22a

Activity

Engage in some bird watching! Try to home in on a flying bird and see if you can follow its flightpath with your eyes. Discuss what you would get up to if you were as wild and free as a bird?

In a quiet moment (perhaps over a picnic), talk about the Holy Spirit. Discuss the story of Jesus' baptism, and how the Spirit descended on him, looking like a dove. Ask if anyone can think of why the Holy Spirit chose to show himself as a dove?

Perhaps it was as a symbol of peace and reconciliation (remembering the dove in the story of Noah's Ark)? Alternatively, Jesus also talks about people 'born of the spirit' as blowing like the wind. You cannot tell where the wind come from or where it is going. There's something about the freedom of birds in flight that makes us think of the Holy Spirit, going wherever he pleases. Celtic Christians have been known to call the Holy Spirit "the Wild Goose", capturing something of his untameable nature.

You will need

Binoculars
A good bird watching spot
Bird-spotting book or app

Going Deeper

2 Cor 3:17 says 'Now the Lord is the Spirit, and where the Spirit of the Lord is, there is freedom.' Are there things that hold you back from being fully free in the Spirit? Perhaps you could share these, and pray prayers of confession. Receive God's forgiveness for the things that stop you being free.

Worship Response

Ask God - in the middle of nature whilst bird watching, if appropriate - to come and fill you again with the Holy Spirit. Ask him to lead you in wild and free directions.

Paint or draw the flight paths of your birds

TASTE AND SEE

> *"Taste and see that the Lord is good"*
> Psalm 34:8

You will need
Some edible things found growing naturally outside: berries, herbs, fruit etc

Activity
Use the grid overleaf to describe the foods using every sense; what does they look like, taste like, feel like, smell like and sound like (for example, when you bite it or knock it)?

Talk about how God created us with five senses and that he wants us to worship and explore him with all the senses. Read Ps. 34:8 and discuss what you think the writer meant by using this image.

Next, read 1 John 1:1, and think about what it must have been like for the first disciples, walking around with Jesus, experiencing God with all their senses. Think together about how we can experience God with all our senses today (we can get clues by engaging with his creation in multi-sensory ways), but also how we can serve and worship him with all five senses.

Worship Response
Ask people to think about their favourite food, music, people/pets, smells, and sights in creation, perhaps write them down or draw them. Then they can call them out during this prayer:

Father God,
Thank you that when we eat our favourite foods, like ... we taste your goodness.
Thank you that when we hear our favourite music, like... we hear your beauty.
Thank you that when we touch our pets or hug our families, like... we touch your love.
Thank you that when we smell our favourite scents, like... we smell your creativity.
Thank you that when we see our favourite things in creation, like... we see your greatness.
Help us to taste, hear, feel, smell and see your glory all around us.
In Jesus' name, Amen.

Food:				
Looks like:				
Tastes like:				
Feels like:				
Smells like:				
Sounds like:				

WHY SHOULD CHRISTIANS CARE ABOUT OUR PLANET?

Since you've picked up this book, perhaps you are already convinced that caring for the earth is an essential part of living a Christian life. Yet for many churches, the environment is something that gets mentioned only very occasionally, if at all. It gets treated as an optional extra for people who are into that sort of thing. And that is a shame, because the earth has as much to offer the church as the church has to offer the earth.

"In the beginning, God created the heavens and the earth" (Gen 1:1). So the Bible begins, with a poetic story of God lovingly shaping a beautiful world, and then filling it with creatures to share it with him. We learn that it was carefully crafted. Genesis describes God organising the universe and setting its rhythms in motion: the 24 hour cycle of the day, the month long lunar cycle and our year-long orbit around the sun. The earth is tilted on its axis by 23 degrees, which is why we have seasons. Asaph didn't know that when he wrote Psalm 74, but he was quite right to sing "yours is the day, yours also the night. You established the moon and the sun. You have fixed all the bounds of the earth. You made summer and winter." (Ps 74:15-11)

God made the earth to be shared. After he created the seas and the dry land, God issues a series of invitations. Let the earth produce vegetation, let the water bring forth life. "God who fashioned and made the earth," says Isaiah, "did not create it to be empty, but formed it to be inhabited" (Is 45:18). And he got what he asked for: a vibrant, colourful, buzzing world, full of life at every scale, from the tiniest microbes to the mighty blue whale.

Creation was not a one-off event. Genesis tells us that God made the stars, but we know that stars are still being born today,

somewhere in the universe. It tells us that God separated the land and the water, but the tectonic plates are still moving, and mountain ranges are still rising. The same is true of living things. When God called life into the seas, the land and the air, he created a dynamic process of evolution that would move towards ever greater beauty and diversity.

Like any work of art, the earth tells us plenty about what its creator is like. God's fingerprints are all over his world. "The skies display his craftsmanship" as David sang in Psalm 19, while Paul argues in Romans (1:20) that God's nature is so evident in his creation that people "have no excuse for not knowing God." If we want to know what God is like, we will find our answers in God's two revelations – the person of Jesus described to us in the Bible, and creation.

So here we have this earth, created with care and made to be shared, an ongoing creation that declares the glory of God. And what does God do with it? He gives it away. As Psalm 115 says, "the heavens belong to the Lord, but he has given the earth to all humanity."

Ultimately, the earth is a gift. God gave it to us as our home. When you think about it, that should be reason enough to take the environment seriously. If the earth is a gift from a loving creator, who made it in lavish diversity, is it okay that so many species are going extinct on our watch? If God shaped the earth so carefully to give us the perfect conditions for life, is it okay that we are changing the atmosphere and warming the planet? Of course not, because that dishonours the gift of creation. Genesis tells us that the things God made are good, and when we pollute a river or destroy a creature's habitat, we're essentially saying that they are not. We're making our own judgement – this thing is not good, it is worthless.

Environmental destruction is an insult to God's creation, but it's also a really dumb thing to do, because we live here! God gave us the earth as our home, and we all know we should take care of the places where we live. We fix a leaking roof, try to keep our homes clean. It becomes an inconvenience, even a danger, if we don't. The earth as a whole is no different. And it matters that we think about the earth as a whole, because often the environmental damage from our consumer choices falls in faraway places, and on people who contributed little to the problem.

Caring for the earth is pretty common sense really, but perhaps one of the reasons we don't think about it is that we don't actually engage with creation very often. Most of us live indoor lives, and nature is something we go and visit when we feel like it. When we do see it, it's often in contained and domesticated forms, like a city park. If we live in an urban area, it might even feel like nature is deliberately kept at arms' length,

concreted over and fenced off. It doesn't surprise us or delight us, or even cross our minds very often. So we forget about it, and the damage that humanity is doing to the environment gets forgotten too.

As we engage with nature, our awareness of the life all around us will grow. We will notice more, open ourselves up to wonder again, and learn to see the world as God sees it. The earth will speak to us about God, and we will spot new ways to "tend and watch over" it, as God asked us to do in Genesis 2. That's where the rest of this book comes in.

The world is intricate and diverse, offering great opportunities to discover its wonders and dive deep into its mysteries. God made it to be shared, so let's explore it together as families, with friends, and with the Creator himself. It's an ongoing creation, which means we don't just get to go and look at it, we get to participate in it. And it points us to God, which is an invitation to seek him in it and praise him for it.

So what are we waiting for? Let's get our boots on...

... AND 10 WAYS TO START

Here are ten starting points, or ways in to caring for the earth. They're not tips or a to-do list, but avenues to explore, and you can go as deep as you like down any of them. Have a browse, and see what you feel invited into.

1. Keep learning

Get to know your world. Learn to identify birds, insects, trees, cloud formations, stars, the phases of the moon. The more you can recognise around you, the more points of connection you will have with the world and the more rooted in creation you will feel. Investigate what interests you. And who knows, you may stumble on a life-long passion in the process.

2. Show hospitality

We share the world with all manner of creatures, from the harmless bacteria that live in our digestive tract to the big trees at the end of the street. Jesus told us that a sparrow doesn't fall to the ground without God knowing about it (Matt 10:29), so showing hospitality to the creatures around us isn't going to go unnoticed either. Put up bird boxes, build an insect hotel, plant a bee-friendly garden. Resist the suburban dream of a perfect lawn and leave the chemicals in the shed.

3. Grow something

We are a part of the environment, and partnering with the earth to produce something together is the best reminder of that. Start with whatever you've got – a windowsill or a balcony if need be, and get some herbs, chillies and tomatoes growing. Dig up some lawn and build a raised bed or two. Make a herb garden. Plant a fruit tree. Grow salads in pots on the patio. If you're not really the gardening type, plant things that'll come back every year with minimum effort, like rhubarb or raspberries.

4. Leave the world better than you found it

It's what your Grandma told you to do and she wasn't wrong. Sow wildflower seeds on empty or abandoned land nearby. Do some guerrilla gardening. Volunteer with conservation groups to plant trees or improve your local park. If you're out for a picnic or a walk, bring a bag and pick up some rubbish.

5. Get to grips with your carbon footprint

If all the two billion Christians in the world took responsibility for their carbon footprint, we'd be well on our way to solving global climate change. Calculate your carbon footprint online, and go to work on it as a household. Insulate your home to the highest level. When you replace appliances, buy the most energy efficient. Walk or cycle, and try to avoid driving. Don't fly unless you have to. Look for opportunities to reduce your energy use wherever possible.

6. Live more simply

One of the biggest causes of environmental destruction is the endless quest for more stuff – more clothes, more toys, more gadgets. Instead, repair and refurbish. Buy secondhand. Stick with that mobile phone one year longer. Choose fewer, higher quality things. Look for creative ways to pass on anything that's no longer needed. Learn contentment, and discover just how many forms of wealth there are beyond money.

7. Think about what you eat

Life in the natural world has a rhythm to it. We can tap into those rhythms again by eating more seasonally. It has a far lower ecological impact, and also happens to be cheaper and tastier too, as you'll be eating everything at its ripest and freshest. We should also consider eating less meat and dairy, as these are major causes of deforestation and climate change. Look for meat with high animal welfare. There is a time for everything, as Ecclesiastes says, and that includes a time for a really good steak!

8. Shop ethically

We get to vote for the kind of world we want every time we go shopping. Consider your spending as an opportunity to support the things you believe in. Buy local when you can. Buy Fairtrade. Support artists and craftsmen and cottage industries. Look for clothing labels with good ethical practice, and detergents that are kinder to aquatic life. Choose a bank account and investments that reflect your values.

9. Bring up children to love nature

If you have kids, bring them up with an appreciation of nature and an understanding of its value. Explore the natural world together. Learn new things. Go foraging. Get muddy. Most of the things on this list are more fun with children involved anyway, and probably easier too. You can tap into your children's desire to learn and reawaken your own curiosity in the process. Children who love being outdoors will grow into environmentally responsible adults, and that's one way of leaving the world better than you found it.

10. Talk about it

Model ethical living without judging, and you'll inspire others to see what they can do. See if you can improve recycling rates or energy efficiency in your workplace. Support school growing clubs. See if there's a Transition Town or other local initiative you can join - we can do so much more in community, and it can be lonely without a few like-minded people around us.

Jeremy Williams is a writer, project developer and freelance journalist. He lives in Luton and blogs at www.makewealthhistory.org

'HOMIE' - A SAFE PLACE

> "He is my refuge and my fortress, my God, in whom I trust"
> Psalm 91:2

Activity

Play a game of tag. The person who is "it" must choose something to be "homie" before each round of the game, that is; something that the players can touch in order to stay safe from being tagged. Homie could be something like any tree, stone or colour, or perhaps to make it more challenging, a particular kind of tree (eg. birch).

"It" calls out, for example: "this round, homie is any birch tree, 1 2 3", and at that point tries to tag people. The aim for the rest of the players is to find 'homie' to hold on to as quickly as possible. The first person to be tagged is 'it' in the next round.

After the game, ask everyone to describe what homie is and does; how does it feel when you can't reach it in time? How does it feel when it's easy to get to? Discuss how the Bible says that God is a bit like homie, he is a refuge that we can run to and be safe. Psalm 46:1 in the Message says: "God is a safe place to hide, ready to help when we need him."

You will need

A varied space to play tag in, woodlands are ideal

Going Deeper

Read Psalm 91:2 and try to memorise the line "He is my refuge and my fortress, my God in whom I trust." Talk about what "refuge" and "fortress" means, and perhaps try to think of actions that will help you remember the verse.

Take turns sharing life circumstances where group members need God to be a fortress at this time. Pray for each other.

Worship Response

Look around your environment; what looks like the safest thing around? Talk about why it looks safe, for example; stones are hard, trees are tall, the building looks solid and so on. Go and lean against the safe thing you've spotted, and pray something like "Thank you God that you're a safe place to hide, a bit like this [stone/tree/house etc], but stronger, safer and bigger. Help me remember to come to you when I'm scared. Amen." If you memorised Ps 91:2 your could also repeat this verse.

A HIDING PLACE

> *"But Jesus often withdrew to lonely places and prayed."*
> Luke 5:16

Activity

Start this activity with a simple hide and seek game. Make clear how far away players are allowed to go. If playing with children outdoors, keep a couple of adults out of the game with their eyes open to see where people hide.

After the game, get together and talk about the hiding places: Which hiding place was good? Why was it good?

Explain that Jesus often hid outdoors to pray. The Bible says that he went off by himself to pray (Luke 5:16), and that he often did this outdoors, on a mountain (6:12). Discuss why you think that Jesus made a habit of going to pray by himself?

Talk about how nice it is when you have been rushing around, feeling stressed, or been at a noisy gathering; to come home into a quiet room. Explain that Jesus had lots of people crowding in on him all the time, but he knew it was important to pray to Father God, so he had to "hide" to be able to focus.

You will need

An outdoor space with many hiding places

Going Deeper

Discuss: Where do you think Jesus would have withdrawn to pray if he had come to our time and area? What are good solitary places around where you live?

This might be especially challenging if you live in a busy city, or share a house with many people, so help each other come up with creative ideas.

Worship Response

Ask everyone to find a hiding place to pray (keeping within the previously laid boundaries). Encourage each person to pray to God from their heart in their solitary place, and also to give time to just be quiet and see if anything pops into their mind that might be from God. Gather together after a few minutes and let anyone who wishes to share - did they enjoy being alone with God? Did anyone hear anything from God?

BALANCING ACT

> "Cast all your anxiety on him because he cares for you."
> 1 Peter 5:7

Activity

Walk across the log a few times until everyone has had a go. Talk about how life can sometime feel like a balancing act, where we are worried that we're going to slip up or take the wrong step. Sometimes we don't help things by adding worry to our lives.

Get a volunteer to balance on the log, and get your "worry items" out. Ask the group to suggest things that people might worry about, eg. school results, whether someone likes you or not, friendship break-downs, someone saying mean things about you, work pressures etc.

For every worry that is suggested, assign this worry to an object (or write it on a box) that you give to the balancer to carry. See what happens to the balancer the more objects they have to carry. Discuss that life also gets more wobbly the more worries we carry.

Introduce the concept that Jesus wants to carry our worries, and help us walk a more balanced life. Learn 1 Peter 5:7 "Cast all your anxiety on him because he cares for you."

You will need

Something to balance on (a fallen log is ideal, but you could also make something with a few bricks and a plank)

Some items to represent worries (could be things like sticks that you find in the woods, or cardboard boxes that you can write the worries on)

Going Deeper

Let everyone write a secret letter to God about the things they worry about.

They can then scrunch it up and carry it during the worship response (do not forget to pick them up and throw them away after!).

Worship Response

Ask each person to spend some time in silence and to think of a worry that they currently carry. Let everyone choose an object to represent this worry, then hold it whilst balancing on the log. Read the verse to the person on the log and encourage them to throw their "worry" away and find better balance.

Take pictures of your balancing and stick them here

SHEPHERD'S VOICE

> *"...his sheep follow him because they know his voice."*
> John 10:4

Activity

Play a game of animal sounds on an empty field or meadow: pair people up and give each pair an animal that makes a recognisable sound (for extra challenge or an older group, make each pair a different kind of bird).

Put a blindfold on one partner in each pair, and ask all the blindfolded people to stand together. Quietly scatter all the non-blindfolded people equal distance away, leaving the blindfolded people in a huddle in the middle. On the count of three, allow the pairs to start communicating, using only the noises of the animal they were given. First pair to reunite wins!

Talk about what was difficult and what was easy about the game. Did you find each other because you listened to the animal sound, or did some of you recognise your friends' voices?

Jesus says that he is our shepherd, and he keeps us safe because we can recognise his voice.

Why is it important for us, like sheep with the shepherd, to know Jesus' voice? What are some ways we can hear the voice of Jesus - through the Bible; a sense in our heart; through the words of a friend...?

You will need

A large field or meadow to play in

Going Deeper

Talk about your experiences of trying to hear the voice of God. What gets in the way? What is helpful?

Share stories of listening to God.

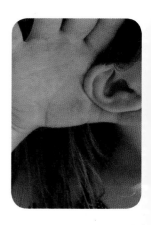

Worship Response

Spend some time lying down on the grass in silence, and ask God to speak a word of encouragement to each of you. Give enough time, then get back together to share.

Note down anything you heard from God

BE STILL AND KNOW

> *"Be still and know that I am God"*
> Psalm 46:10

Activity

Play a game of "Grandma's footsteps". For this, one person is "Grandma" – they face a tree or wall with plenty of space behind them. The others in the group start at the other end of the space, or at a designated spot, and try to creep up to Grandma and tap her on the shoulder.

However, at any moment, Grandma can turn around suddenly. If she sees anyone moving that person must return to the start. No-one is allowed to move while she is watching them. Whoever manages to tap her on the shoulder becomes Grandma and the game starts again.

Talk about the challenges of the game. What was the best strategy? When was it difficult?

Read Psalm 46:10 "Be still and know that I am God." How does being still help to know God?

You will need

Space to play

Going Deeper

Discuss: What in everyday life stops you from "being still and knowing God"? What kinds of things get in the way?

Use the columns overleaf to note these down. Next, help each other come up with ways and strategies to be still in everyday life.

Worship Response

Spend some time "being still" and focusing on God together. Get comfortable, and close your eyes or look at something simple like a flower, a tree or a candle. You can encourage people to repeat a name of God (Jesus, Lord, Holy Spirit, Friend) in their mind to help concentrate. If you get distracted by a thought or movement, don't be discouraged. Just recognise it, put it to one side and turn back to the name. Simply "be" in God's presence.

Person:				
Gets distracted by:				
Ideas for them to be still in everyday life:				

SMELL LIKE JESUS

> "For we are to God the pleasing aroma of Christ among those who are being saved and those who are perishing."
> 2 Cor. 2:15

You will need

Strong smelling perfume
A clean rag

Activity

Play a smell treasure hunt - soak a piece of cloth in a strong smelling perfume and hide in a small area. See if the group can find the cloth using their sense of smell. Take turns hiding the cloth.

Explain that animals in the wild use their sense of smell, like we just did in the game, but for them it is not a game. They need their sense of smell to find food, to avoid dangers and find members of their flock. Would you be able to find your family members by just using your sense of smell?

Explain that the Bible describes Christians as "the pleasing aroma of Christ" in the world. This does not mean wearing some special perfume, but improving the atmosphere and changing the environment of where we are - what are a few ways in which we can do this?

Extra Fun

See if your group members are able to spot what is edible using only their sense of smell: fill five jam jars with different things, blindfold the volunteers and see if they can sort the edible from the inedible by smelling the contents of the jars.

Some good things to put in the jars could be: coffee, vinegar, chocolate, gingerbread, curry paste, banana, any herbs or orange segments/peel, and perfume, washing powder, TCP, washing up liquid, new cut grass or soil. You might want to throw in a jar of Marmite as a joke! N.B. be aware of any allergies present in your group before planning this.

Worship Response

If everyone has had a go at hiding the rag, they should be able to smell their hands and sense that their hands smell of perfume too. Ask everyone to smell their hands and pray something like this: "Dear Jesus, please help us smell of you when we walk around in your world, help us to be more and more like you and improve our environments by our presence. Amen."

Scribble ideas for being the aroma of Christ here

CONSIDER THE LILIES

> *"...And why do you worry about clothes?*
> *See how the flowers of the field grow..."*
> Matthew 6:28

Activity

Enjoy this activity when you find yourself somewhere with lots of wildflowers.
Jesus says: "See how the flowers of the field grow", or in the King James version "Consider the lilies..."

Spend some time considering the wildflowers; talk about their different colours, how their petals are shaped, how many petals they have, how tall they grow, what their leaves look like, if their stems are thick or thin. Sketch the flowers or photograph them.

Whilst everyone is drawing, read Matthew 6:28-34 out loud. Explain that Jesus asks us to look at nature to get a better perspective on our worries and concerns. We need to trust that he will provide for us, and seek to get to know him better.

You will need

Flowers to look at (preferably wildflowers)
Pens and paper

Going Deeper

Discuss:
1) Do you worry about things like food and clothes, or other things?
2) In what way do you think seeking God could help with these concerns?

Share tips together on how you deal with worries. Remind one another of how God has provided and been faithful in situations that have worried you in the past.

Worship Response

Share the things you worry about, and then consider how God provides for the flowers. Pray a prayer giving your worries to Jesus, say for example "Dear God, I give my worry about [something] to you. Help me trust that you care for me even more than you care for this flower."

As a reminder, ask everyone to write "Jesus cares" around the flowers they sketched earlier.

Draw or paint your wildflowers here

MINI-WORLDS

> "These commandments that I give you today are to be on your hearts. Impress them on your children. Talk about them when you sit at home and when you walk along the road, when you lie down and when you get up." Deuteronomy 6:6-7

Activity

Children and adults alike enjoy miniature worlds (just visit the mini-world at Legoland if you need convincing). Children especially process much of their learning about life by playing with mini-worlds such as Lego, Playmobile, dolls' houses etc.

With a little imagination, things found in nature can make up the elements in a mini-world; perhaps a stone looks a bit like a house, a particular stick like a horse, and a pine cone with some twigs poked in can be a person?

After reading any Bible story, try to process it by playing it in a mini-world. The classic story to make is the Easter story. There is a description of how to make an Easter Garden in the Engage Lent Journal, downloadable from our website.

Adults might help by asking questions like: "How do you think that person felt at that time?", "What happened next in the story?' or "What do we learn about God here?".

You will need

Objects found in nature, eg: pine cones, sticks, weeds, stones, etc

Going Deeper

If you make an Easter Garden, as well as making Jesus out of pipe cleaners or sticks, make a representation of yourself too.

Then share with each other where you would place yourself in the garden; do you feel a need to reflect on the cross, confessing sin and seeing Jesus pay the price? Or are you waiting with expectancy by the tomb, hoping for God to do the impossible in your life?

You can do similar things with any other story you play - placing yourself within the scene.

Worship Response

In the process of playing the Bible story, you might think of a characteristic of God that stands out - his love, faithfulness, forgiveness etc. Pause and thank God for that side of his nature towards you.

Make a list of the Bible stories you could re-create as mini-worlds, and how to make them

GOD IN CONCRETE

> *"Seek the peace and prosperity of the city to which I have carried you into exile. Pray to the Lord for it, because if it prospers, you too will prosper."* Jeremiah 29:7

You will need

Cameras or smartphones
An urban space

Activity

Go on an urban safari in a built-up space. Take photos of "glimpses of God" amongst the concrete, cars and bustle. These might include:

- unexpected (and possibly unintended) examples of beauty and peace;

- places where humans have used God's gifts creatively, with skill and wisdom;

- cross-shapes that happen naturally in things like brick, shadows, spaces, trees;

- other signs of God you notice when you begin to see the area with heavenly eyes.

Going Deeper

You could also look for signs of where God is needed. Be a bit more careful what you take pictures of at this point - avoid being rude or intrusive. But you may be able to capture some images which you could take back to help you pray for the area.

Worship Response

When you get back, print out the pictures or put them into a PowerPoint presentation or a video loop.

Look at the photos and have a time of prayer for the area. Pray for the prosperity of that place. Thank God for signs of him which can be found everywhere.

Write down what you discovered on your walk

DEN BUILDING

> "Live in temporary shelters for seven days: All native-born Israelites are to live in such shelters so your descendants will know that I had the Israelites live in temporary shelters when I brought them out of Egypt. I am the Lord your God." Leviticus 23:42-43

Activity

Build a den together! In the woods, collect loose sticks (never break off from a living tree) and lean against a fallen tree or big rock. In the garden put a sheet over some branches, or over a table.

When Israel left Egypt and wandered in the desert for 40 years, they all lived in tents, which could be packed up and carried with them. Even God's presence received a dwelling place, a tent which was called "the tabernacle". The feast of "tabernacles", or sukkoth, was celebrated to remember where they had come from, and the people were encouraged to build a den to live in for the duration of the festival. Many Jews still do this today!

Sit in your den and talk about what it must have been like to live in tents for 40 years. Read John 1:14 and explain that this verse is about Jesus coming to earth, "tabernacling" with us - or as it says in The Message version, he "moved into the neighbourhood". This is a vivid image of how Jesus really knows what it's like to be human.

Going Deeper

Prepare some information in advance about people who still have no permanent home. Try to find some images of some of the large refugee camps, and imagine what it might be like to live like that.

Discuss how Jesus was a refugee to Egypt as a child. He later said "Foxes have dens and birds have nests, but the Son of Man has no place to lay his head." (Matt. 8:20). Jesus knows what life is like for refugees and displaced people. Spend some time praying for people like that.

Worship Response

Take turns to think of one thing that can be awkward and uncomfortable about being a human (eg. being hungry, tired, the chafing of uncomfortable shoes etc.) and pray saying something like: "Thank you Jesus that you know what it's like to feel [insert word]. Amen."

Stick photos of you in your den here

JESUS IN THE BOAT

> *"Then he got up and rebuked the winds and the waves, and it was completely calm."* Matthew 8:26b

Activity

Make boats out of bark or walnut shells. Let everyone use their imagination and think about what makes a good boat. When everyone is finished, test them out in the sea, on a pond or even in a paddling pool - did they float?

Read the story from Matthew 8 (you may want to act it out together).

Talk about what they must have felt like stuck in the storm (if your little boat capsized earlier, you may want to imagine what it would have been like to have been a tiny passenger on that boat). Which words would you use to describe what the disciples must have felt like after Jesus calmed the storm?

You will need

Bark from dry, dead wood or walnut shells
Anything to decorate your boats (for example, lollipop sticks and cloth to make sails)

Going Deeper

Share any storms that people are finding themselves in at the moment, and pray for God to be present with them in the midst of the storm.

Worship Response

Ask everyone to close their eyes and imagine together:

"Imagine that your life is a boat, sometimes it sails along nicely, the sun is shining and everything is going well - when did you last have times like that?

"Sometimes the ride in the boat of your life turns bumpy, you see dark clouds and it seems difficult to steer through the high waves - when did you last have times like that?

"However we feel, it is always better to have Jesus in the boat with you. Take a moment to invite Jesus to step into the boat of your life. Imagine that he steps in - what does that feel like?"

Talk together about what you imagined, and pray for each other.